Rob Versus
The Whackadoos

Conquering Ridiculous Attitudes and Scammy Behaviors With Lightning Fast Wit & Shearing Sarcasm.

Rob Anspach

Rob Versus The Whackadoos

Conquering Ridiculous Attitudes and Scammy Behaviors With Lightning Fast Wit & Shearing Sarcasm.

ISBN 13: 978-1-7377355-1-9

Printed in USA

Disclaimer:
Oh yes, we must have a disclaimer…it makes the lawyers happy. The author has spent a lifetime using sarcasm as a means to grow his business. He shares interactions in this book that you may or may not agree with, his actions and communications are contrary to what most customer service gurus teach. But, it works for him and could work for you too, although highly doubtful.

What People Are Saying

"In the beginning of this book, Rob claims it has been 2 minutes since he was last sarcastic. If ever there was an algorithm that 'rounded up', it's that one. He sets his own boundaries, and is successful because he obeys them. What could have been a distraction has become a comedy gold mine, as the rest of the world keeps tapping on the glass to get his attention. Because of him, here are 3 things I know to be true:
1. *Rob is the most prolific dead person I know.*
2. *His brain is more valuable than coffee.*
3. *When it comes to Whackadoos, Rob is never gonna give you up, never gonna let you down."*

~ **Steve Gamlin** - The Motivational Firewood™ Guy

"As I read Rob's latest book Rob Versus The Whackadoos, I found myself trapped liked many of his scammers who can't help themselves from responding. I couldn't stop reading anticipating the next great scam of the scammer. Rob Anspach does what so many of us wish we would do when we are accosted by these time wasters. Once again, "Rob Versus..." wins and the scammers lose." ~ **Brett M. Judd**, Success Mastermind & Personal Mindset Coaching - http://www.theapexeffect.com/

"Upon receiving my preview copy of Rob Versus The Whackadoos, I printed it out to make for easy reading. While reading this book, a yellow jacket wasp flew into the window by my chair. So I rolled up the manuscript I had printed out and proceeded to whack the yellow jacket before it could sting me. Although after reading this book, I have wonder... Was it the blunt force trauma or Rob's sarcasm that killed the wasp?"
~ **Paul Douglas**, Titan Marketing, Winnipeg Manitoba (coauthor with Rob on Optimize This: How Two Carpet Cleaners Consistently Beat Web Designers On The Search Engines 2014, Revised 2018)

"I pissed myself laughing at this on the plane ride back from LA!"
~ **Brandon Straza**, The Success Finder, www.TheSuccessFinder.com

"The book is AWESOME! Just when I think I have read it all, here comes more. Each of these books get funnier seeing how they respond to Rob's sarcasm. I look forward to each new book. In addition to having a good laugh they can be educational about all the scams people face every day. Thanks Rob for educating and entertaining us". ~ **David L. Brown**

"At some point or another, every entrepreneur and business owner deals with a few Whackadoos. Despite your screening processes and all the times you've been once bitten to become twice shy, a few slip through the net regardless. It's an occupational hazard. In his inimitable sarcastic and humorous way, Rob Anspach speaks for all of us by sharing his own stories from the trenches. Read this book. Enjoy Rob's stories. Within them, you will find subtle yet priceless lessons on how to optimize your mindset so you effectively serve your community, market, and audience from your intersection of your brilliance and your passion!"
~**Adam Hommey** - Creator, The R.E.A.C.H. System
https://www.TheReachSystem.com/

"It was an honor to be able to give a review for this book. Rob Versus the Whackadoos, yes, I read it. And kept reading it. Odd thing is, one of his Whackadoos examples called me the next day after reading the chapter with the same story, and thanks to Rob, I had the perfect answer. I memorized it. And I am not joking. And it was fun to go back at this Whackadoo and make him realize that scammers will not overwhelm me. And that sarcasm has its place in chosen situations."
~ **LaurieAnn Campbell**, www.IAmThatGal.com

"Rob Anspach has done it again! And "Whackadoos" doesn't do justice to the inept fools who somehow manage to find Rob. Only Rob Anspach could turn phone calls from idiots into a profitable business! While teaching us how to handle and have fun with these sad little people. He should thank God for creating so many people to play with! Buy it, and all of Rob's other books. I treasure mine!" ~ **Ben Gay III**, The Closers

"My uncles were all farmers. In their outhouses, they had a book shelf. They always said, "Think, don't stink." I think that is why all my cousins have good jobs, happy marriages, and excellent health. Growing up, I remember sitting there, reading a Reader's Digest from their bookshelf. I loved "Quotable Quotes", "Life's Like That" and other columns full of short stories. Rob Versus the Whackadoos is like Reader's Digest for the 21st Century, full of stories that you can read during an outhouse visit. I love that Rob takes some time at the end of each story to share his experience and wisdom. It is must reading for anyone wanting to avoid the heartbreak and expenses of the world's top scam artists. Everyone needs to get multiple copies, put up a shelf in their washroom, and change the world." ~ **Scott Paton**

Read more reviews at the end of the book. ☺

Table of Contents

Introduction

Hi, I'm Rob and it's been 2 minutes since my last sarcastic remark. I know what you're thinking…that type of behavior shouldn't be tolerated. And I would have to agree. Two minutes is a long time to go without using sarcasm. Maybe my powers are slipping?

Nah.

As you'll soon discover from this book (which incidentally is book 5 in the Rob Versus series), I use sarcasm as my weapon of choice to conquer those that would waste my time, create situations that irritate me or try to scam me in some way, shape or form.

Welcome to "*Rob Versus The Whackadoos*".

Bigger. Bolder. Faster. Stronger.

Well, I don't know about all that. It's a book. It's filled with funny stories. Read it. Smile. Laugh. Share.

What I do know is that once you learn the dark art of sarcasm your life will never be the same. I can attest to that. I can't go anywhere without someone doing or saying something to trigger my sarcasm.

Oh, and I want to thank Adam Hommey, Gerry Oginski, Mia Oginski, Courtney Beauford and Kirt Christensen for contributing their stories to make this book even better.

I guess I should also thank all the scammers, spammers time wasters, morons, and fools who made all the rest of the stories possible. But I won't.

Anyhow…

Enjoy the book.

And if you haven't read the first four books in this series, the links to order are in the back of the book. Please order a bunch, and when I say a bunch, I really mean a couple hundred copies. Give them to anyone who appreciates sarcasm.

Rob Anspach

AnspachMedia.com

P.S.
"If you just read the "Notes" at the end of each section, you'll thank Rob for all of the brilliant, actionable, real-life advice. But then you'd miss out on the non-stop hilarity in all of his stories. So don't do that."
- **Steve Sipress**, Small Business Growth Expert

Chapter 1

My Facebook Friends

"Not really my friends…
but without them, this book wouldn't happen."

Did You Listen?

I received an audio message from a new connection on Facebook. I didn't listen instead I responded...

Me: ?

Them: Did you listen to my message?

Me: No!

Them: Why not?

Me: I prefer to read messages not listen to them.

Them: That's stupid.

Me: Yes I agree sending a new connection an audio message is very stupid indeed.

Them: Would you take a minute and listen to the message?

Me: Just tell me what it's all about.

Them: Listen to the message.

Me: I can't, it's too noisy here.

Them: Put headphones on.

Me: So not only do you want me to listen to a message you could have just typed but now you want me to put on headphones to listen to that message, shall I make funny faces as well? Maybe dance around too?

Them: Are you always this rude?

Me: Not always...but today's your lucky day.

Them: All this could have been avoided if you just listened to the message.

Me: Oh yes, it's my fault.

Them: Will you listen to the message now?

Me: Nope.

Them: Why not?

Me: You didn't say the magic word.

Them: This is ridiculous.

Me: Nope that's not it.

Them: OMG.

Me: Not it either.

Them: F-You.

Me: Not even close.

Them: A-Hole.

Me: You're not even trying anymore.

{and he blocked me}

Note: I know a lot of people just love to press a button a record a voice message…I'm not one of them. I prefer emails, chat messages and texts. Why? I can read faster than most people can talk. Especially when they drone on and on when leaving an audio message. And, when I start to think "good gawd…are they still talking" then the message is too long and absolutely could have been a text, short chat message or even an email. Plus a non-audio message can be read everywhere. But a voice message definitely can't be listened to in most places where others may be present.

WTF Indeed

Hey Rob I see we have 400 mutual friends.

{message I received on FB chat}

Me: Apparently so.

Them: Well that's creepy.

Me: Okay.

Them: Did you friend request all my friends so I would eventually connect with you?

Me: Why did you send me a connection request then?

Them: I wanted to see who you were and why 400 of my friends were connected to you.

Me: Well, why don't you ask them.

Them: That just seems stalkerish to me.

Me: Hmm, how can I be a stalker when you requested the connection and I accepted?

Them: That we have 400 mutual friends speaks volumes.

Me: Yes, it means they like me better.

Them: WTF!

Me: Yes WTF indeed. You're crazy.

Them: I'm blocking you.

Me: And the trash takes itself out.

Them: What does that even mean?

Me: Are you blocking me or what?

Them: I want to know why you just called me trash.

Me: And you're paranoid and need medicated too.

Them: I'm reporting you to Facebook.

Me: Whatever floats your boat.

{and I got blocked}

Note: I've been on Facebook since 2009 and reached Facebook's 5000 friend limit a few years ago. Occasionally, I delete non-engaging friends to make room for new connections. And I never accept connections with ZERO mutual friends. Most of the time that new connection has hundreds of mutual friends which makes it easier to say YES. But to accuse me of stalkerish behavior before I even accept your friend request makes this person a prime whackadoo.

Arguing With Pitas

So the other day I read a post from a Facebook connection who said "don't trust anyone who asks for money upfront".

To which I replied, *"without payment I don't start the work"*.

Them: That's how people get ripped off .

Me: That's right, me!

Them: I won't pay anyone upfront.

Me: Sounds like contractors need to avoid you then.

Them: They are all crooks.

Me: Maybe you're the crook.

{well, that was the trigger and the convo escalated to FB chat}

Them: Yo dude, what's your problem? Why did you engage my post if you're just going to argue?

Me: I posted how I do things, you made it into an argument.

Them: You seem like a pompous ass.

Me: Yup, but I get paid upfront.

Them: Not from me.

Me: Nope, you're not a good fit.

Them: Why, because I won't pay up front?

Me: No, because you're a PITA.

Them: A what?

Me: A Pain In The Ass.

Them: So that's what that means, and no I'm not.

Me: Sounds like you've been called that before.

Them: F-You.

Me: I'll take that as you have.

{And I got blocked from chat and unfriended}

Note: As a business owner getting paid quicker should always be a priority. Most businesses do not have the ability to go 30, 60 or even 90 days without payment. Why should they anyway? They have labor, equipment, insurance and other expenses that need to be paid. So I say get paid upfront and eliminate 90% of the hassles right away. And those that don't want to pay upfront can go somewhere else.

Chapter 2

Is It Me You're Looking For?

"Apparently not…but I made the best of it."

The Amazon Phone Scam

My mobile rings...it's from 1800-673-3094

{I know it's a scam...but you know me, I have to answer}

Me: Hello.

{Automated message: Your bank account has been successfully linked to your Amazon Pay, please press one to speak to a representative.}

Them: Hi Sir, your Amazon account is pending a charge for $1499 for an iPhone 11 are you ready to place that order?

Me: iPhone 11? Hmm, I don't recall ordering that...but I did order a throat punch machine, do you see that on the order?

Them: Sir, did you not place the order?

Me: Ah, no! Why would anyone spend $1499 on a iPhone 11 when ATT is charging just $10 a month for them?

Them: Sir, are you saying you didn't authorize this purchase?

Me: Yeah, that's what I'm saying.

Them: Okay Sir, we will need your Amazon account information and your full name to proceed.

Me: You called me...you should have that information already.

Them: No Sir, we only get your number to call you to inform you that a charge of $1499 for an iPhone 11 is pending against your account.

Me: Well, go ahead send the phone and I'll just send it back.

Them: No Sir, we can't do that, we need your Amazon information and then we can stop the iPhone 11 from being shipped out.

Me: I don't want the phone, but do want the throat punch machine.

Them: Sir, you don't understand.

Me: Sure, I understand.

Them: That is what, Sir?

Me: That this call is bogus, and all you're trying to do is get my Amazon information.

{You would think he would have hung up but nope.}

Them: Sir, without your Amazon account information we can't stop the iPhone 11 from shipping and a charge of $1499 being applied to your Amazon Pay which can't be contested.

Me: Well, I'm not giving you my account, so go ahead and ship the phone and yes I will be contesting it.

Them: But Sir, you will be charged $1499 aren't you concerned?

Me: Nope.

Them: Sir, we really need your Amazon account information.

Me: Well, I really need that throat punch machine...looks like we are both shit out of luck.

Them: No you are shit out of luck.

Me: Yup, guess I am.

Them: No iPhone 11 for you.

Me: I didn't order it anyway.

{and I got cursed out in some foreign language and he hung up }

Note: Almost every household on this planet has an Amazon account. And, getting a call from what seems like Amazon informing you of charges you weren't expecting can seem overwhelming. These calls are most likely scams designed to steal your credit card information. Don't fall for it.

Philip From The Warranty Center

Hi this is the Warranty Center press 1 to update the coverage on your vehicle.

{me pressing 1}

Me: Hello

Them: This is Philip with the Auto Warranty Center can you please give us the make, model, mileage and year of your vehicle. {says super-fast}

Me: Can you slow down a bit so I can understand you.

Them: This... is... Philip... with... the... Auto... Warranty... Center... can... you... please... give... us... the... make,... model,... mileage... and... year... of... your... vehicle.

Me: Can you say it slower please.

Them: This...... is...... Philip...... with...... the...... Auto...... Warranty...... Center......

Me: Slow isn't working for me, can you go back to fast.

Them: Sir are you wasting my time?

Me: Can you say that in Spanish?

{He hung up}

Paul From US Home Solar

My cell phone rings – caller ID screams it's a scam...you know me...I have to answer.

Hi this is Paul from US Home Solar offering a free solar consultation...is this the person responsible for paying the electric bill?

Me: It is.

Caller: Can I ask who your electric provider is? Is it PPL, PECO or something else.

Me: HWP

Caller: Thank you Sir... can I ask who that is?

Me: What you never heard of HWP? It stands for Hamster Wheel Power and it's really the next gen compared to solar.

{the caller paused and I thought he would hang up, but he didn't}

Caller: Well Sir, I'm sure we can save you money on our solar package.

Me: Maybe, probably less smelly too.

Caller: Sir, does your roof get good exposure?

Me: I dunno, never went up to check.

Them: Does it get enough sunlight.

Me: It's a roof, I have no idea.

Caller: Do you live at {surprisingly gives correct address}?

Me: No...that's not correct.

Caller: Can you give me your correct address so I can pull you up on Google Maps.

Me: So you give someone's address in hopes I will give you my correct address, then you'll probably use the address I give you to scam someone else out of giving their address?

Caller: Sir, that is not how it works.

Me: Well it sounds like how it works.

Caller: Well we need your address first, then we look at the Google map to see the neighborhood...

Me: And to see how close the nearest police station is right?

Caller: Sir, can you give us your correct information so we can proceed?

Me: Nah, I don't want you giving my address to someone else or Google mapping me and seeing where I live.

Caller: We will find you.

Me: Sounds like a threat.

{they hung up}

Note: If you receive a call from a fast talking salesperson or someone you just don't know, never acknowledge the information they give to be yours. Saying, "yes that's correct" could be all they need to create a fake account under your name or capture your data for nefarious reasons.

D and B Score Lending Scam

Received call on a spoofed number...

{I didn't answer}

Michael leaves a message telling me based on my company's Dun and Bradstreet score they can lend me $500k at 4.9% then leaves a number for me to call back.

So I return the call...
the person who answers doesn't identify himself by name, then says the person who reached out is on the sales team and doesn't know all the ins and outs of commercial lending.

Me: And your company name is?

Them: We are a commercial lender that helps businesses get the financing they need.

Me: Well that's a very long business name.

Them: Oh no, that's not our name, that's what we do. We will gladly share the name of our company once we get additional information from you. We need to see if you're a right fit.

Me: Then I'm probably not a good fit.

Them: Well, to get started and to determine if you're a good fit we need 6 months of your bank statements.

Me: No can do, I don't reveal information like that.

Them: Well that's the only way we can determine if you are right fit.

Me: Like I said I'm probably not a good fit.

Them: Why did you call us?

Me: I wanted to know how this scam worked.

Them: F-You it's not a scam.

Me: If you have to say F-You when defending yourself then it's definitely a scam.

Them: F-You

{and he hung up}

Note: Never hand over your bank statements to random callers. And seriously if the person calling doesn't identify themselves… it's a scam.

Chapter 3

Bueller, Bueller?

"Pardon my French, but you're an a$$h*le."

Irritated By My Reply

Hahahaha... you think you're so clever with your out of the office email auto reply...pfft...not clever enough apparently.

Them: Rob why did you keep responding to my auto-reply. It clearly states I will be out of the office over the weekend.

{message I received thru Facebook chat}

Me: Oh, I read that. But I wondered how many responses I could send that would trigger you to finally contact me over the weekend. And the answer is 7.

Them: 7 huh? I didn't count. Do you need something?

Me: No I got my answer.

Them: So that is all you wanted? To find out how long it took to irritate me into responding to you?

Me: You call it irritate I call it an experiment.

Them: You evidently aren't busy enough.

Me: It was the weekend...I needed something to do.

Them: F-You!

Me: So next time will you respond to me faster?

Them: I just won't engage the email autoresponder the next time I want a weekend off.

Me: Mission accomplished.

Them: F-You!

Me: You seem irritated, you should really learn to relax.

{and I got blocked}

Note: Email auto replies can create more headaches than they are worth. Especially to people like me. Oh, but you know what's fun…activating your own "autoreply" and letting it reply to the other autoreplies. Yup, did that a few times to people and within a few hours they had about a hundred messages in their inbox of just an endless loop of autoreplies. Good times.

Ferris Was A Stupid Movie

Grr...I've gotten 3 emails in a row all starting off with...

"I hope you're well and in good health."

Then they proceed to tell me about what they are selling.

So being the nice guy I am...I just had to reply...

Here's what I sent them...

"Um, yeah I'm sick. I guess your best friend's sister's boyfriend's brother's girlfriend heard from this guy who knows this kid who's going with the girl who saw me pass out at 31 Flavors last night. I think it's pretty serious."

To which I received from one emailer..."*we will remove you from our list immediately*".

The second emailer replied with...

"Ferris? That was a stupid movie. You need to grow up. In fact, don't bother ordering we are blocking your email."

I haven't heard from the 3rd emailer yet.

Note: Ferris Bueller's Day Off is an awesome movie that everyone should see about 100 times to appreciate.

Quantum Email

Hey Rob, did you get my email?

{message received through Facebook chat}

Me: When did you send it?

Them: 15 minutes ago.

Me: I check my email in the morning, after lunch and before I close down for the evening...not every 10 minutes.

Them: Could you check it now?

Me: Since you are already sending me a chat here, tell me what your email is all about.

Them: Could you just check your email?

Me: Again, I check my email in the morning, after lunch and before I close down for the evening...not every 10 minutes.

Them: So you're not going to check your email now.

Me: NO.

Them: I don't understand why you won't just look at my email.

Me: Okay for shits and giggles and to get you to stop bugging me I will look.

Them: Good.

Me: I don't see it.

Them: Well I sent it.

Me: Did you?

{10 minutes go by}

Them: It was stuck in draft just resent it...please look now.

{waiting 10 more minutes before checking}

Me: Still nope.

Them: It's got to be there.

Me: Looks like it went to the junk folder.

Them: Well it's not junk.

Me: Gmail thinks it is, so it must be.

Them: Did you look at it.

Me: Nope, it's junk.

Them: DUDE, WTF!

Me: What is it about?

Them: The email?

Me: No we were talking about Quantum Clustering using the idea of time-independent Schrödinger equations.

Them: What?

Me: Yes, you dingbat, the email. And no, not reading it. Probably not ever now.

{wait for it...}

Them: F-You then.

{and I got blocked}

Note: I find this scenario plays out time and time again by those who are trying to sell me on the newest get rich quick scheme or some multi-level marketing recruitment blitz. It's always annoying. And precisely why I don't check email every 10 minutes.

Chapter 4

Nothing But Scammers

"As far as the eye can see…scammers everywhere!"

I'm Only Weird To Spammy Callers

Phone rings...

Caller ID displays "Sekure Merch So"...

You know me I answer it anyway...

Me: Hellooo.

Them: This is Asia with Sekure Merchant Solutions, can I speak to the person responsible for your credit card processing?

Me: Oh, he got fired.

Them: Well is there anyone else I could talk to?

Me: Well let's see... Mike quit, Suzy is in jail, Dewayne went missing, Stu is drunk again and Phil is...

Them: Sir, I'm looking at your team members on your website and none of them match the names you just said...are you pulling my chain?

Me: We update the names on our website in real time.

Them: I don't believe you.

Me: Well I don't believe you are who you say you are either.

Them: We are a credit card processor and we sell credit card processing services.

Me: I'd rather talk about the chains you believe I was pulling. What are they made of? What color are they? How heavy do they weigh?

Them: No wonder people quit, get fired, go missing, get drunk and go to jail... you are weird.

Me: Bwahahahaha.

{the caller hung up}

Note: You might be thinking, "hey they could be a legitimate company and the caller is just trying to do her job". Maybe! But then again they could be a scammer trying to get my credit card information. Why take a chance?

Scammer Threatens Me With Death

Another day...another scam call.

Me: Hello.

Them: This is Diane from Red Senior Benefits.

Me: Who?

Them: {says even louder} This is Diane from Red Senior Benefits.

Me: I'm neither deaf nor a senior.

Them: Well, we are offering a death benefit that covers the expense of dying; such as your funeral costs, casket and other needs.

Me: I don't need a casket, maybe just a cardboard box or a giant trash bag or something.

Them: No joke, you're going to die so you might as well plan for it.

Me: Do you know when? I think that would be more helpful than your death benefit.

Them: We know where you live.

Me: Oh I see...you're threatening me then.

Them: Sir you live at {gives address about 40 miles away}

Me: That's right come on over, we'll have some tea and talk about your scam.

Them: {screams} You're going to die. {then hangs up}

Note: Yup, eventually I will die. We all will. And funeral planning is of course something we should all consider. But I'd rather deal with my local funeral planning services than someone on the phone who is a stranger to me.

Getting Scammed By The Beatles

Phone rings...my caller ID says it's a SCAM.

Pfft - you know me...

Me: Hello.

{slight pause and then a click}

Automated message comes on... "*Hi this is Billie with Green Energy calling to see if we can help you lower your electric rate consumption and put more green back into your pocket...press 1 to continue.*"

Me pressing one. A guy speaking with an Indian accent named Paul answers.

Paul: Hi, this is Paul and I see you pressed one to learn more about our special deal.

Me: Mmm, yeah.

Paul: Are you the proud owner of your single family dwelling?

Me: You could say that.

Paul: That is great, you qualify.

Me: Cool, I never qualified for anything before, this is so exciting.

Paul: Okay Sir, what electric provider are you currently with?

Me: HWP! {which stands for Hamster Wheel Powered, but he didn't ask}

Paul: Oh yes, we do collaborate with that company, and can negotiate a great term for you.

Me: Really? Well, that's fantastic.

Paul: Do you receive any discounts?

Me: Discounts?

Paul: Such as senior citizen discounts?

Me: How old do you think I am?

Paul: Sir it's an example. I have no idea how old you are.

Me: So why did you use that as an example?

Paul: Are you going to let me finish my script?

Me: I don't know, are you going to call me old again?

Paul: I don't like you? I think I will end the call now.

Me: Don't quit now, I need to know how you will collaborate with my electric provider.

Paul: F-You.

{Paul transfers me to George who's accent is very hard to understand}

George: You need to stop wasting my trainees time if you have no intention of buying.

Me: You need to stop wasting my time and everyone else's time with your scam.

George: F-You Mother F-er.

Me: You really need to use your real names... George? Paul? Really? I bet there's a Ringo and a John working there too right?

George: There is what of it?

Me: Hahaha...they are the names of the British Rock Band, The Beatles.

George: Never heard of them...now stop wasting our time.

{He hung up}

I was about to sing him a verse from ... *"Can't Buy Me Love"*.

Note: If they collaborate with a made up electric company, they're scammers. And seriously I don't trust anyone who hasn't heard of the Beatles.

The Scammer Said I Lied

Phone rings...Caller ID displays
"C Rock from Houston TX"

{me thinking yeah right, it's a scam}

{but you know me...I answer it anyway}

Me: Hello.

Them: Your Social Security Number has been compromised, please press 1 to talk to an agent.

{so I pressed 1}

Agent: This is Dan from Social Security {he says with a thick foreign accent}

Me: Hi Dan, someone called me and said my social security was compromised.

Agent: And you pressed 1 for more information correct?

Me: Apparently so.

Agent: Could I get you name?

Me: {uses the name associated with the Caller ID) C Rock

Agent: Why lie?

Me: Me lie, never!

Agent: Our records show you are Rob Anspach.

Me: Never heard of him.

Agent: Sir, you are Rob Anspach.

Me: If you know who I am, why ask for my name?

Agent: We want to make sure you are the right person before we reveal more information.

Me: A scammer who cares, how nice?

Agent: Sir I didn't catch that, can you repeat.

Me: Sure, you're a scammer, trying to scam me...you don't work for Social Security, and you're probably calling from some call center in Pakistan.

Agent: F-You.

Me: Pakistan it is then.

Agent: We will get your information.

Me: {me impersonating Rocky when he goes up against the Ivan Drago} Go for it!

Agent: F-You.

{and he hung up}

Note: If the caller ID doesn't match who is calling…it's a scam.

Chapter 5

Absurd Rudeness

"And darn proud of it."

Rules Of Phone Scamming

Phone rings...yup it's a scammer.

I answer anyway.

{Recorded message says… *"This is Ashley from the Card Services Division of Visa/Mastercard here to offer you an approved interest rate of 0% for 18 months - press 1 to speak to our representative today"*}

So I pressed 1.

Scammer: I see you pressed 1 to take advantage of our lower rates.

Me: Yup.

Scammer: Can I know the card with the high balance?

Me: Sure, but first whom am I speaking to?

Scammer: I'm Kevin from Card Services.

Me: Wow, that's a long last name.

Scammer: What? No, I'm from Card Services, that's not my last name.

Me: Okay, whatever...how do I get this deal?

Scammer: What is your card with the highest balance? Is it a Visa or Mastercard?

Me: Mastercard.

Scammer: What is the expiration date of that card?

Me: Why?

Scammer: We need to know if it's still valid.

Me: It is, I just used it this morning...still works fine.

Scammer: Can you tell me what the expiration number is?

Me: Well, can you share with me your card information first?

Scammer: Sir, what do you mean?

Me: Well if you want me to share with you my information, I think it would be prudent to share your information with me first. You know to build trust.

Scammer: I don't have a Mastercard.

Me: Well how about your Visa, or Discover or Amex? You got those right?

Scammer: Sir, I don't have any credit cards.

Me: Why not? Why are you working for Card Services if you don't have any credit cards?

Scammer: F-You!

Me: Hahahahahahaha.

Scammer: Why are you laughing?

Me: If you're going to scam me, you got to learn how to play the game, son.

Scammer: We will get your information eventually.

Me: Doubtful.

Scammer: F-You.

Me: First rule of phone scamming, don't curse at the person you are calling, that's a dead give-away that you're a scammer.

Scammer: F-You.

Me: Second rule of phone scamming, if you fail the first rule at least learn more than one curse word.

{pfft, he hung up...apparently he doesn't like my rules or how I play the game}

Note: Never, ever verify the expiration date or your credit card numbers to a random caller.

What's A Good Number?

Phone rings - caller ID says it's a spoofed number.

Yet I answer it anyway...hey it's what I do.

Caller: Hi this is Brad with Cheaper Insurance (dot) com and we would like to save you money on your car insurance. Would that be of interest to you?

Me: Yeah, not really.

Caller: Great, I will have an agent call you in a bit and review with you our great rates, would that be acceptable?

Me: No, not really.

Caller: That's awesome, what's a good number for the agent to call you back on?

Me: 911

{and the caller hung up}

Note: Most scammers use an automatic dialing program that calls hundreds of numbers a day. When they call you, most times, they have no idea what your number is. But by answering their "what's a good number" question they can add your verified number to future scam calls.

Unknown VOIP Seller

Phone rings...Caller ID displays "Unknown".

Well you know me, I have to answer.

Me: Hello

Caller: Is...s...ob? {sound is very crackly}

Me: Your sound is horrible and I'm having a hard time hearing you.

Caller: Please...old...n...I'll...itch..ines.

{there is a pause}

Caller: Is this better? {now it sounds like he's under water}

Me: Not much.

Caller: Let me try something else.

{there is a pause and he returns}

Caller: How's this?

Me: Sounds better, what did you do?

Caller: I switched headphones.

Me: Okay...what can I do for you?

Caller: I'm calling from Apex Technologies about our newest VOIP system.

Me: You're serious right?

Caller: Yes, our VOIP system has many new features.

Me: Yes, I experienced those when I picked up the phone.

Caller: You did?

Me: Dude did you fall down and hit your head?

Caller: What?

Me: You called, the sound was crackly and then it sounded like you were underwater, then you had to switch headphones.

Caller: Oh that's my phone, nothing to do with the VOIP system.

Me: Don't you think you would use that system to sell that system?

Caller: They don't give us the system to use.

Me: Well, then no I don't want to know more.

Caller: May I ask why not?

Me: You can ask me.

Caller: Okay why not?

Me: I did say you can ask me, but I don't have to answer.

Caller: What da' f?

Me: Yes, that's how I feel about this call too.

Caller: Why did I even call you?

Me: Do you want a simple answer or shall I give you some new age esoteric philosophical bullshit?

{pfft...he hung up}

Note: If the caller isn't using what they are selling, good chance it's a scam.

Call Me Westley

Phone rings... Caller ID displays "Scammer"

You know me...

Me: Hello?

Caller: Hi I'm with Green Energy Electric, may I ask your name.

Me: I formally went by DP Roberts, now retired.

Caller: Okay may I call you DP?

Me: No, call me Westley.

Caller: Okay Westley, are you in charge of paying your electric service.

Me: Yes, I assumed that responsibility from the prior DP Roberts who assumed it from the gentleman who held the position before him.

Caller: This sounds familiar.

Me: Inconceivable.

Caller: Is your wife by chance named "Buttercup"?

Me: No, but I knew of a Buttercup.

Caller: You're a liar!

Me: I am a man of action. Lies do not become me.

Caller: This is absurd...why are you wasting my time.

Me: I hope this doesn't put a damper on our relationship.

Caller: What you talking about?

Me: Life is pain. Anyone who says different is trying to scam you.

Caller: I'm not a scammer.

Me: Nonsense, you only say that because no one ever has.

Caller: I'm hanging up.

Me: As you wish.

{and I had so many more Princess Bride quotes to use on that caller}

Note: If they're going to call me and try to scam me, I might as well have fun responding to them by using quotes from my favorite movies.

Technobabble

Phone rings... Caller ID Displays "Spam Risk"

...and I have to answer it. It's what I do.

Me: Hello.

Caller: Hi we would like to introduce you to the newest in home alarm technology.

Me: What kind of technology?

Caller: Our systems cover Motion, Breakage and Smoke.

Me: Do they have Trellium-D subspace connections with multiadaptive processors?

Caller: Sir? I'm not sure what you said.

Me: Do you know its progressive pulse compression wave output number?

Caller: Mm, ah, er...

Me: Does it come with magnesite-nitron phaser polarity with paraphoretic photon launchers?

Caller: Sir, I don't think our system does any of that.

Me: Is it built with nitrium autocompositors with the temporal subspace frame.

Caller: I don't think that technology exists.

Me: Well I need the system to have self-sealing holo-dampeners with docked memory crystals.

{slight pause...then}

Caller: F-You and your Star Trek technobabble.

Me: Live long and prosper!

{they hung up}

Note: Hey they called me...why do they get so upset when they don't like what I have to say?

Rick Rolling A Scammer

Caller ID...displays "Scam Likely"
...but you know me...I just have to answer...

Me: Hello.

Hi this Daniel from Discover Card Services.

Me: Okay.

Daniel: I'm calling to offer you a Zero percent interest.

Me: I already get a Zero percent interest.

Daniel: Our rates stay at zero. We will never let you down.

Me: Will you run around and desert me?

Daniel: Sorry what?

Me: Will you make me cry? Will you tell me lies and hurt me?

Daniel: Sir, I have no idea what you are saying.

Me: You know the rules and so do I.
A full commitment's what I'm thinking of.
You wouldn't get this from any other guy.

{pfft he hung up}

Dumbass

Somebody called me this morning three times from the same number.

I didn't answer.

They didn't leave a message.

They then emailed me saying how they tried to call me.

After I didn't respond to email, they sent me a direct message through Facebook.

Me: You called, emailed and now are direct messaging me, what is it you want?

Them: We want to help you.

Me: Apparently you are the one who needs help.

Them: We noticed you don't answer your calls, or emails.

Me: I do that for a reason.

Them: And that is?

Me: My time is valuable and I don't like wasting it dealing with people who are intrusive, or who want to sell me on how they think they can help me.

Them: How do you get clients if you don't answer the phone?

Me: They find me.

Them: Same way we did then?

Me: No, they respect my time, you don't.

Them: You're rude.

Me: Rude is calling someone multiple times and never leaving a message. Rude is emailing someone to tell them you called and then direct messaging them when they don't respond to email.

Them: You don't get it.

Me: Oh, I get it just fine, you're a dumbass who doesn't understand how to help a potential client - you just think calling, emailing and direct messaging is the thing to do.

Them: Dumbass?

Me: Yup.

Them: You're a jackass.

{He blocks me from replying}

Then sends me an email saying how rude I was.

Then he blocks my email.

Beetlejuice

Hi this Steven calling to offer Final Funeral Expenses information.

Me: I died last year.

Steven: Sir, we can have someone call you back in the next 24-48 hours to review options.

Me: Options? Are you going to bring me back to life?

Steven: What?

Me: I'm dead.

Steven: How are you answering the phone?

Me: I haven't crossed over yet.

Steven: Then you need our services.

Me: Nope, got it covered.

Steven: I can have a representative contact you.

Me: Beetlejuice, Beetlejuice…

{pfft…he hung up}

Chapter 6

Simply Ridiculous

"And it's probably a good idea not to ask for my opinion."

Use Your Brain

"Hey Rob I'd love to pick your brain over coffee."

{message received thru FB messenger}

Me: Well that's one way to ruin a coffee.

Them: What?

Me: I'm sure what you meant to say was you'd love to get my opinion while meeting at a coffeehouse.

Them: That's what I said.

Me: How about you set up a 30 minute paid phone consultation with me and you can drink coffee if you wish.

Them: Well I don't want to pay.

Me: Well I don't want to offer you my services for free.

Them: What's your rate?

Me: {quotes rate}

Them: F-that!

Me: Do you still want my opinion?

Them: Yes.

Me: My opinion is… you should pay the rate and schedule a consultation.

Them: You're an ass.

Me: So is that a yes to the consultation or a no because you're cheap. I mean "you're an ass" could go either way.

{pfft, I got blocked}

Note: Your time is worth so much more than a coffee. And if the person requesting to meet doesn't want to pay for your knowledge they're not a right fit.

Ridiculous Attitude

Last Month...

"Rob we would like to take over our social media and have our team post from now on."

Me: Do you have a strategy that you'll implement to ease the transition?

Them: No, but we think we can do it.

Me: Fine, I release you. Good luck.

This Month...

"Rob we need help, apparently our team doesn't know what they are doing and only posted 3x since last month."

Me: Well, here's my price to take you back.

Them: WTF - that is more than double.

Me: Yup.

Them: Why?

Me: If you want my help, that's the price.

Them: We don't want to pay double.

Me: Well, you made the mistake of thinking your team could do what we've been doing for the last 2 years.

Them: Yes, sorry...but double?

Me: That's the current price for new clients.

Them: We are not a new client, we are an existing client.

Me: No you are a previous client who didn't value our service and since more than 30 days have gone by you are now considered a new client and thus the new price.

Them: That's ridiculous.

Me: What's ridiculous is your attitude. So I'll make it easy for you and tell to look for another service, I'm not interested in taking you back for any amount of money.

Them: F You.

Me: Oh yes, that's a prime way of trying to convince someone that you are worthy.

Them: We are not paying double.

Me: No, you are not paying anything, we are not taking you back.

Them: F You.

{and the person blocked me from replying}

Note: There should always be a penalty for taking a client back. Why? You will have to fix all the stuff they or another service screwed up.

Invisible 12 Pack

Was at Wegmans Market and as the cashier was scanning our groceries the monitor displays "Mello Yello 12 pack".

I say I didn't buy any Mello Yello.

Cashier says, "what's Mello Yello?".

I say, "it's soda, made by Coca Cola."

Cashier looks at me and says, "I don't drink soda."

Me: Okay, good to know, why did it show up on the scanner?

Cashier: Already removed it.

Me: Yeah okay, but why did it show up?

Cashier: Don't know, don't drink the stuff.

Me: Yup, you already said that.

Cashier: Do you need another cart, you have a lot of groceries?

Me: No.

{Cashier looks at the other employee and instructs her to get us another cart.}

Me: We put everything in one cart.

Cashier: You're a one cart-er!

Me: Yup, with my invisible Mello Yello 12 pack.

Note: Logic escapes some people, use it to your advantage. However, be prepared to be challenged by those with no sense of humor.

Impossible Order

My wife and I were returning home from a dinner out with friends and we get a text from our daughter asking us to pick up an Impossible Whopper at BK.

So I pull up to the BK drive thru order taking machine...

"Welcome to BK can I take your order?"

Me: Yes I would like to order an Impossible Burger meal.

{the order taker screams to the crew..."do we gots any of those Impossibles?"}

Order Taker: Yeah I'm not sure we have anymore impossible burgers I am checking.

Me: We heard.

{We hear over the speaker…"do we have anymore Impossibles", "huh, oh we do"}

Order Taker: Okay we have some, anything else?

Me: Fries and a Coke.

Order Taker: That'll be $11.90

{Me staring at the menu...seeing the Impossible meal price as $7.99 plus tax.}

Me: Why $11.90? What I ordered is your number 3 for $7.99 plus tax.

Order Taker: Well that's not how you gave it to me.

Me: I said the meal.

Order Taker: I will fix your mistake.

Me: What?

Order Taker: Pull around to window one Sir.

{I pull to window 1}

Person at Window 1: That'll be $9.78

Me: What?

Person at Window 1: You ordered the Impossible Meal with large fries and soda.

Me: Grr...I ordered it regular size, but whatever.

Person at window 1: Okay Sir here's your change pull up to window 2

{Pull up to window 2 - then waited 3 minutes}

{finally someone comes to window...I could tell by the attitude it was our order taker}

Order Taker: Here's your food {basically shoving it at me}

Me: Thank you.

Order Taker: Here's your drink {the lid not being secure, and me trying to grab hold so as not to spill it into my car.}

{The order taker disappears before I could look up to say thank you...or kiss my ass as I wanted to say.}

Note: About a week later, my wife and I happened to be in the area and stopped at the same BK. A different crew was working this time. And although they took the order correctly, when I got to the first window and asked for a receipt they said the person at the second window would give it to us. Well, I get to the second window and I see receipts being printed out. Then a crew member crumbles up all the receipts. Hmm, I thought that's weird. So I ask for my receipt. And the person at the window says, sorry the printer is broken. Grr.

Here's My Number, Ask For Jenny

At the auto parts store and they are ringing up my purchase…they ask for my phone number.

Me: I'd rather not.

Clerk: Well Sir, we can't process the purchase without a phone number, policy Sir.

Me: Well that's a stupid policy.

Clerk: We do it to protect you.

Me: How is having my number protecting me?

Clerk: Sir, do you want your items?

Me: Yes, but I'm not giving you my number.

Clerk: Well I need someone's number to get a hold of you if there is a problem.

Me: Fine...here's my work number 867-5309 ask for Jenny first.

Clerk: Thank you Sir. Here's your items.

{me humming the lyrics to the Tommy Tutone song as I leave the store}

Not Joking

"Hey Rob"

{message received in my FB chat}

"Hey Rob"

{message received 20 minutes later from another person through FB chat}

{phone rings...caller ID matches name of first person who sent chat...let it go to voicemail}

"Yo Rob"
{message received on LinkedIn from second person who messaged me on Facebook}

Play voicemail..."Hey Rob, I see you are on Facebook but you didn't reply to my message, I want to hire you for a project."

{Me going to Facebook replying to message} "You typed HEY ROB like that was supposed to get me to reply right away, why not tell me what you needed through chat?"

Get reply: Oh, I suppose I could have done that, sorry. Please disregard the message I sent using my friends account and also the LinkedIn message too.

Me: Good gawd...do you even know how to be patient and wait for a reply?

Them: I got you to reply didn't I?

Me: Well just for that I'll be charging you.

Them: That doesn't seem fair for getting your attention.

Me: Which took me away from another project I was working on.

Them: Well then you have time to chat.

Me: Before we continue I'm sending you an invoice for $1500 after you pay it, we can continue.

Them: You're joking right?

Me: Yes, of course $1500 is too low, make it $2500

Them: What is your problem?

Me: You're right...$2500 is still too low, $5500 should do it.

Them: F-that.

Me: I think it's rather fair since there is like four of you sending me messages.

Them: No just me using several names.

Me: Yeah, I'm not into helping someone with a split personality.

Them: Do you always treat people like this?

Me: Only those with multiple identities.

{yup, and it was then I was blocked on Facebook, LinkedIn and though the phone company.}

Note: This type of whackadoo will suck the joy out your life. And, even if you charged them 100x more than your normal rate it wouldn't be worth it.

Circular Conversation

Hey Rob, we don't know each other, but I notice we move in the same circles. Let's connect, if you're open to it.

{message received through LinkedIn}

Me: Circles? I'm more of an ellipse type of person.

Them: What the actual F*ck!

Me: What? You don't know what an ellipse is?

Them: IT'S THE SAME THING AS A CIRCLE!

Me: See this is why we can't be friends, you are shouting already and don't understand the difference between a circle and an ellipse.

Them: THIS CONVERSATION IS OVER, YOU'RE INSANE!

Me: Well clinically I've never been diagnosed, but you may be right...but then again you notice people moving in circles.

Them: STOP REPLYING!

Me: See this conversation isn't over.

Them: LOOK YOU DUMBA$$ STOP REPLYING

Me: It sounds like you need anger management, I'd be happy to contact someone for you...I'll even ask if they like circles.

{phone rings}

Me: Hello

Them: Look you dumb shit stop replying to my LinkedIn message.

Me: Wow, you are angry.

Them: Dude, you have no idea who I am.

Me: Apparently you're someone who likes circles.

Them: F-YOU, MOTHER F-ER.

Me: Well this was fun, let's have another circular conversation tomorrow, okay?

{he hung up, then blocked me on LinkedIn}

Note: Some people get triggered by the littlest things...isn't it great. Winning friends and influencing people is literally the opposite of what I do.

Chapter 7

Budgetary Concerns

"If you have to ask, then you probably can't afford me."

Asking For A Budget – Part 1

Hey Rob, you never asked me what my budget was, like all your competitors did?

Me: I never ask prospective clients what their budget is, nor do I care. I give them my price and it's up to them to come up with the money. Oh, and I have no competitors.

Them: What do you mean you have no competitors?

Me: Some people may do what I do, to some extent...but they will never do exactly what I do in the manner I do it.

Them: Sounds like semantics to me.

Me: Sounds like you need to keep looking then.

Them: But we want to hire you.

Me: Nah, too late. Not interested.

Them: Is this some reverse-psychology make us want to hire you even more marketing technique?

Me: Nope, just me doing what I do in the manner I do it.

Them: Well, we could have been a great client.

Me: That's debatable.

Them: That's rude.

Me: Is it though?

Them: Yes, I'm trying to hire you and you don't want to accept it.

Me: That's my choice isn't it.

Them: Well, we would never turn away a client.

Me: And that's why I can't accept you as a client. You are not capable of understanding why a business needs to be more critical on who they accept as clients.

Them: We never say NO to a prospect or a client.

Me: Well, I'm saying NO to you.

Them: I think we got off on the wrong foot, can we start over?

Me: Sure...Hi this is Rob...we are not accepting clients like you at this time.

{wait for it...}

Them: F- You!

Note: There is no other person who does what you do in the manner you do it. That's your superpower.

Asking For A Budget – Part 2

Hey Rob your post about the guy with the budget post actually had a legitimate question and you dissed him and didn't let him hire you, that's such a bad move.

Me: And who promoted you to KING?

Them: Well nobody but it's common courtesy to ask for a budget?

Me: Says who?

Them: Everyone.

Me: I think you have me confused with someone who has no clue how to run their business.

Them: How do you even have customers?

Me: Well I run my business the way I want for starters.

Them: That's stupid.

Me: How so?

Them: It's not normal.

Me: Have you met me?

Them: Well I think you should be nice and ask for a budget.

Me: Okay let me fill you in on 2 very important things...

(1) I don't give a shit what you think and

(2) Those who ask for a budget usually pigeon hole themselves into finding a solution to work within that budget, meaning they undersell themselves and undervalue the experience they bring to the table.

Them: Well I don't see it that way.

Me: Well you run your business your way and I'll run mine how I see fit.

Them: You would be wrong.

Me: Would I, really? The whole purpose of being an entrepreneur is creating a business built around your personality that allows you to connect to the right people and live your best life.

{apparently he didn't like what I was saying and he blocked me}

Note: It's your business…your rules. If someone wants to do business with you, then they need to play by your rules. Period. No exceptions.

Chapter 8

Write, Read or Listen?

"Yup, three ways I trigger people with my sarcasm."

Random Guy Wants Me To Help ME Write A Book

Hey Rob, I've written 12 books in 20 years and I can help you write your book with my new course.

{message received from some random guy on Facebook}

Me: Hmm, do you even know me?

Random guy: Well not really, but I'm sure you have aspirations of writing a book.

Me: Look at my profile.

Random guy: Oh, you've written a few books it seems.

Me: More than a few yes...over 30 in 8 years.

Random guy: Well I think you could still benefit from my course.

Me: I think not.

Random guy: I've helped hundreds of people.

Me: So.

Random guy: I can help you.

Me: I think it's I that can help you.

Random guy: How's that?

Me: By blocking you so you don't bother me again.

{wait for it...}

Random guy: F-You!

Note: Don't you just love when random people reach out to sell you on their service when you have more experience and knowledge then they do? That's a rhetorical question. I already know the answer. That would be a NO!

Congrats, or Not!

"Hey Rob, congrats on the new book."

{message received in LinkedIn messaging}

Me: Did you read it?

Them: No, just saying congrats though.

Me: Are you going to read it?

Them: Maybe I'll listen to it if it's on Audiobook.

Me: Then you won't.

Them: Won't what?

Me: Then you won't read it?

Them: Why not?

Me: Did you eat a bowl of lead paint chips for breakfast?

Them: What the hell kind of question is that?

Me: Oh, so apparently you can read messages on LinkedIn and comprehend the meaning, but you can't read an actual book.

Them: I don't have time to read.

Me: You have time to read this message.

Them: What is your problem?

Me: Which one?

Them: What?

Me: I have many problems, can you be specific?

Them: Can you stop bothering me?

Me: You initiated this conversation by reaching out.

Them: I was being polite and friendly.

Me: That's debatable.

Them: STOP

Me: GO

Them: STOP

Me: GO

Them: What the hell are you doing?

Me: I thought we were playing a game.

Them: Do you know who I am?

Me: Someone who doesn't like reading books, eats lead paint chips and argues with people over LinkedIn messaging.

Them: Not even close.

Me: Really? Apparently your brain hasn't comprehended this whole conversation which you started.

Them: I'm reporting you.

Me: To whom?

Them: To LinkedIn.

Me: Good luck with that.

Them: Again, you have no clue who I am.

Me: Really? I believe I have already established who you are.

Them: STOP replying to me.

Me: Does it bother you?

Them: YES.

Me: Good.

Them: You're a jerk.

Me: Is that the best ya got?

Them: I'm not replying to you.

Me: You just did.

Them: Stop replying to me.

Me: Okay.

Them: You replied.

Me: Looks that way.

Them: Stop it.

Me: Did you report me yet?

Them: STOP replying you A-Hole.

Me: Are you annoyed?

Them: I'm beyond annoyed, you've wasted my time.

Me: Well maybe you will learn from this and not send someone a congrats message for a book you refuse to read.

Them: F-You.

{it was then he decided to unfollow me and block me}

Note: My books are easy to read. I design them that way. So when someone tells me they have no time to read, I have to question their logic.

Rob Anspach

Chapter 9

Not E-Hero Worthy

"In fact, not anything worthy."

I'm Saying No

Hi Rob, I've listened to a few of your E-Heroes podcast episodes and think I would make a great guest.

{message I received thru Facebook chat}

Me: {looking at their profile and shaking my head no...but wanted to see where it would go} Okay.

Them: So you want me on your show?

Me: No I said okay acknowledging your message.

Them: Okay well I charge to be a guest on podcasts

Me: Then, NO!

Them: I don't understand? Why Not?

Me: Well you reached out to me and now you want to charge me to be a guest on my show. It doesn't work that way.

Them: Well if you want me on the show then I charge for my time.

Me: And I suppose you want the questions in advance so you are prepared?

Them: That's right.

Me: No, no and no.

Them: I'd be glad to reduce my rate.

Me: Even if you reduced it to zero, and eliminated the questions in advance I would still say No.

Them: I don't understand, I would be perfect for your show.

Me: Actually no you wouldn't.

Them: Well f-you!

Me: And now you will never be on my show.

Them: You're a jerk.

Me: Oh yes, the "you're a jerk" response always helps seal the deal right?

{and I got blocked}

Note: It was this exact conversation that prompted me to add this script to my podcast page.

I don't accept unsolicited requests to be on my podcast. The only way you will appear on my podcast is if:
(1) I personally invite you or
(2) someone that's been on the podcast suggests I reach out.

I Was Born This Way

Hey Rob, I heard your interview on that podcast.

{message received in the other folder on Facebook...you know the one where non-friends leave messages}

Me: Which podcast? My E-Heroes podcast or one of the many I was a guest on?

Them: Don't remember...but you share how being sarcastic has gotten you more clients and made your more money over not being sarcastic.

Me: Yup, it has.

Them: Can you be more specific?

Me: So apparently you didn't listen very well to the podcast.

Them: I was in my car listening.

Me: Really? What kind of car is it?

Them: A Toyota something.

Me: And what time of day or night were you listening in your Toyota something?

Them: It think it was around 11 at night.

Me: Were you drinking?

Them: Why all the questions?

Me: Well, you can't remember how you heard about me, you have no idea what model of Toyota you drive and clearly you were driving drunk because you avoided the drinking question.

Them: Do you treat everyone who listens to your interviews this way?

Me: Only the ones who evidently weren't paying attention.

Them: You're a jerk. I'm not listening to your interviews anymore.

Me: I don't think you listened in the first place.

Them: Yes I did.

Me: Prove it.

Them: How?

Me: Tell me the podcast you heard me on.

Them: I don't remember.

Me: Guess you'll have to listen to all of them until you can tell me which one.

Them: How many are there?

Me: Between my E-Heroes episodes and the ones I was interviewed on...there's about 200.

Them: Just tell me which one it is.

Me: How the hell do I know which one you listened to?

Them: Guess.

Me: Dude, just start listening.

Them: That's too many.

Me: Well I suppose you'll never learn the answer to how I use sarcasm to make money then.

Them: Fine, I'll listen.

Me: Figured you might.

Them: I'd better learn something.

Me: I doubt it.

Them: Why do you say that?

Me: You can't even remember what model your Toyota is so I doubt you'll remember what episode my divine answer to your question will be on.

{a day later...he responds}

Them: I listened to 30 episodes and found the answer.

Me: And did you learn something?

Them: Yeah, you're sarcastic.

Me: That's already been established.

Them: Why do you have to be that way?

Me: Well as Lady Gaga says, "I was born this way"

Them: No, why do you have to treat people like that?

Me: Why do you care?

Them: I think you could make more money being nice.

Me: I'm not being mean...just sarcastic.

Them: No, you are mean.

Me: Says the guy who can't remember what he drives.

Them: See what I mean?

Me: Nope.

Them: You are using sarcasm as your defense mechanism.

Me: Oh, so you went from wondering how I make money with sarcasm to trying to be my therapist?

Them: I think you need help.

Me: I think you need to listen to more of my interviews.

{and I got blocked}

*All that and I didn't even get a "F-You". I'm really disappointed.

Note: Sarcasm is a way of life. How can you even debate that? Without sarcasm this book and the whole "Rob Versus" series wouldn't exist.

Chapter 10

Mr. Stafford

"It's who they think I am, who am I to disagree."

Solar Or No Solar

My cell rings...Caller ID displays name of local hospital.

Me: Hello.

{recorded message asks if I want to lower my electric rate and if so I should press 1 - I pressed 5 instead...and a rep answers}

Rep: Hi, who do I have the privilege of speaking to?

Me: What do your records say?

Rep: It says your number is associated with Mr. Stafford.

Me: Then that's who you are talking with.

Rep: The Mr. Stafford on Clearview Dr?

Me: Yup, if that's where your records say I live.

Rep: {slight pause} Okay Sir, I'm looking at your house and you have Solar Panels already.

Me: Are you outside?

Rep: No I am using Google Maps to see your home.

Me: Weird.

Rep: Weird how?

Me: I haven't been up on my roof in several years, but I don't remember ever ordering or having installed solar panels, you sure you are looking at my house and not my neighbor's house?

Rep: Yes, I'm looking at your address and you already have solar panels.

Me: Well, I have no idea how they got there. Can you remove them?

Rep: Sir, why are you wasting my time?

Me: Your company called me, I was responding to the offer of lowering my electric rates and you just want to talk about solar panels, so who is wasting time...I think it's you.

Rep: {curses at me in some foreign language}

Me: So when are we going to talk about my electric rate.

Rep: F-You!

Me: Okay before you hang up will you take a one minute survey on how this call went?

{pfft...he hung up}

Note: Sadly, due to Google Maps displaying detailed pictures of homes it has given nefarious people more information they can use to scam others.

The Dreaded BBB

Phones rings... Caller ID displays... "Potentially spoofed number".

You know me...I just have to answer.

Oh no my Social Security number has been compromised...

Ah, nope not mine...a Jim Stafford who they think I am.

Because, when they asked if I was I said, "*yup*".

And an agent named Jimmy Uma (with a foreign accent) was so kind to tell me that apparently I'm being investigated for money laundering. Also the call was being recorded by the FTC, BBB and the Financial Crime Enforcement Agency.

Although his kindness turned quickly when I said, "*Not the BBB, please don't send the BBB after me.*"

{And I thought this is where he hangs up.}

But then Jimmy asked the question...

Jimmy: Can I have the last 4 digits of your social security number for verification?

Me: {making up 4 digits} 6741

Jimmy: Why are you lying to me?

Me: Say what? Those are my numbers.

Jimmy: You said 6749 - the 9 is wrong.

Me: I said 6741 - no 9, never a 9. What's wrong with your hearing?

Jimmy: Okay. Let's proceed.

Me: As you wish.

Jimmy: Grab a pen and write this information down.

Me: Okay...

Jimmy: Your ID for this call is DNC701089, your Arrest Warrant # is 02954687 and my officer # is 02841997 - now read them back to me.

Me: You lost me after "Your ID for this call is"

Jimmy: You're not taking this serious...your social security number is compromised and you are facing serious federal charges.

Me: Whatever...I'll take my chances.

Jimmy: You'll be locked up.

Me: Oh yes, by the dreaded BBB right?

Jimmy: F-You Mother F-er.

{and he hung up}

Rob Anspach

Chapter 11

Friends Versus Scammers

"Adam, Gerry, Mia, Courtney and Kirt, oh my."

Not Holding Back

(submitted by Adam Hommey)

I'm expecting a follow-up call from the management office because I have a pending service request. I spoke with them in person about it this morning... and I wasn't sure if the call was coming from their office across the street or their main office somewhere in Iowa or whatever. They're weird.

So I actually answered my phone when it rang even though I'm extremely busy here....to hear a very nasty caller telling me I was in big trouble because I was delinquent on payments for my car's extended warranty.

They tried to tell me my car would be repossessed if I didn't pay up - and that I would be arrested if I refused to cooperate.

Well....

One of the few things I DON'T hold back on is sharing how I lease cars that are much more than I actually need, because I've always cared more about having a nice car than having a big house (of which I don't even have one of).

So... I'm pretty sure I don't have an extended warranty on a vehicle I leased last summer that just hit the 8,000-mile mark and that I plan to turn it in on a 2023 edition in 2023.

Anyway....

I corrected them and told them I actually lease a modified Cadillac that has a compartment for storing blood and is capable of firing missiles, and it's currently sitting in the garage at 1600 Pennsylvania Avenue, Washington, DC. I also told them there are three such vehicles with identical appearances and features, only one of them is mine, and wished them luck guessing which one to hook the tow truck to.

This scammer then informed me he was a CIA agent and I was in BIG trouble now - and while I laughed over him figuring out my joke, explained that if someone was going to deal with me for having The Beast towed, it would probably be the Secret Service, or their overlords at the Treasury Department. (Yes, I know the Secret Service is now governed by Homeland Security.)

I guess when I said "Treasury", he used that as a key word to open up another script on his Internet Explorer 6-using 2002 Sony Vaio.

He then told me that he had notified my "local sheriff" who was coming to arrest me for delinquent taxes. (Aside from all the holes in this one, if the law was coming for me, it would be the LVMPD.)

I then proceeded to initiate a conversation about his actual lineage, at which point he said he'd "see me in the committary in jail" and hung up.

(I think he met "commissary", and from my understanding, that's not really a place to hang out.)

Mia: Round 1

(submitted by Gerry Oginski)

I had a scammer call me last weekend and I handed the phone over to my daughter. Having read most of your books, she was fully prepared. It was an Indian gentleman calling from Spectrum to give me better pricing on my phone, Internet and cable.

Not once did he ask where we lived to see if Spectrum provided service to my area (they don't). Instead he proceeded simply to tell us he could do better than what we are currently paying. All he needed was a credit card to process the set-up fee which was $5.95.

I motioned to my daughter to argue with him that the fee was too high. After a little pushback, the guy agreed to reduce the fee to four dollars.

Without even asking for her name, he simply began asking for the credit card number.

My daughter asked "don't you want to know my name?"

He stupidly replied "OK. What's your name?"

She replied "Luz Azzhol." (Say it fast).

When he started to laugh at her name, my daughter expressed righteous indignation and started to yell at him that it wasn't nice that he was making fun of her name.

At that point my daughter couldn't hold in her laughter anymore and then proceeded to tell him what a piece of crap he was for trying to scam people out of money.

She learned from the best.

Mia: Round 2

(submitted by Mia Oginski)

Using the lead from one of your recent "Rob Versus" books, I answered a warranty services call.

Them: What is your first name?

Me: D-I-A

Them: Great, what is your last name?

Me: R-R-H-E-A

Them: Can you repeat your first and last name?

Me: D-I-A-R-R-H-E-A

They hung up.

The nerve of someone like him rudely hanging up when I'm trying to give my information.

Particular Set Of Skills

(submitted by Courtney Beauford)

Cindy: Hello Courtney. This is Cindy are you available at the moment?

Me: Hi! What can I do for you?

Cindy: I'm so tied up right now I would have preferred to call you but can't call you at the moment because I am in a meeting and phone aren't allowed during the meeting. I need you to help me out on something very important right from any store around. Let me know if you can do this.

Me: What's up?

Cindy: I need you to help me get Steam wallet gift card from the store, I will reimburse you back when I get to the office. I need to send it to someone and I need to get it sent ASAP.

Me: For how much?

Cindy: The amount I want is $100 each in 5 copies so that it will total $500. I'll be reimbursing back to you. When you get them, remove each card from the pack and scratch off the silver panel at the back of each card to show the claim code then take a picture of the cards and send it to me here ok.

{2 minutes later}

Cindy: Let me know how many minutes it will take for you to get it.

Me: So here's the problem...I don't have money. But what I do have are a very particular set of skills; skills I have acquired over a very long career. Skills that make me a nightmare for people like you. If you stop contacting me now, that'll be the end of it. I will not look for you, I will not pursue you. But if you don't, I will look for you, I will find you, and I will kill you.

He Just Goes On and On and On...

(submitted by Kirt Christensen)

After seeing a post on Facebook, I was curious and sent a FB direct message...

Me: Hey saw your comment, what's your FB ad strategy?

{an hour goes by}

RF: Great to hear from you Kirt, it's not just a strategy, it's a platform that drives traffic and allows you to earn by not posting or selling products. I'm on NYC time call me via Facebook audio and I'll enlighten you to earning and working smarter online – I'm here now.

{two hours go by}

RF: I can't help you if you don't respond – I responded ASAP Kirt!

Me: Can't today sorry. Any links you send me I'll look at tomorrow.

RF: I have a video on the top of my Facebook page my friend.

{Day 2 - the next morning}

RF: Kirt also watch {gives some URL}Questions just ask / ok teach you to earn your online by not selling or posting products.

{2 hours later}

RF: What product or service are you trying to earn from?

{3 hours later}

RF: There is another great video at the top of my Facebook page.

{6 hours later}

RF: Respectfully my friend if you have no time to reply I have no time to help you – good luck, be well – I thought you were serious about working smart online – be well – I wish you all the very best – no need to reply – good luck.

{Day 3 – midafternoon}

Me: I watched the video on your Facebook profile, thanks! Not for me, I'm a paid ads guy and info-marketer, but thanks. Best of luck.

{you would think this is where it ends…nope}

RF: You have no idea what my platform does – I do paid ads. But you need to throw all the crap about marketing out the window – if you want to earn online then rule #1 stop selling. I have students that earn $300 per week. I have students that earn 6 figures every month – if you were working smart and making money you would not need to reach out to me – I earn 7 figures a month – when you start earning that perhaps I'll take you serious and listen to you

– Good luck be well – you just don't get it Kirt and perhaps you never will – carpe diem.

{apparently his ego prevented him from ending the chat}

RF: Respectfully not sure why you denied yourself the opportunity to speak to someone with 25 years of being in the online trenches – not a very smart move sir – good luck be well – keep grinding.

Me: Respectfully no thanks, best of luck.

RF: You don't even know what you're saying no thanks to – but none of this matters anyway – I'm not interested in working with you – No need to reply – enjoy your business.

RF: {gives thumbs up emoji}

Me: Go back to the start of this conversation…I asked about your FB strategy, you replied with a couple of videos. I watched them, thanks. Not applicable to the path and biz that I'm already in, but appreciate the info.

RF: Yes and if you called me I would share my FB strategy with you Kirt – but you were too busy to speak to me between YouTube and FB ads I run 18-20 ads a day for $2 per ad to $20 per ad spend and I make huge ROI while you're still trying to figure it all out. You refused my free guidance so…bye bye.

Me: Great, more power to you. I've probably spent between $2MM and $3MM on Google ads over the years, never got into FB much. I asked a simple question, you responded with a couple of videos, I watched them, end of story. I'm not going to get on the phone and get pitched your 5 webstore pack, thanks, best wishes.

RF: Google ads are for pickers – YouTube ads is where you earn my friend – I can target a YT ad for $20 get 1 penny views and convert to over $4700 net profit from one simple targeted tube video. While respectfully Kirt, guys like you are still trying to figure it all out – my worst students are students with a marketing background – I spend too much time trying to get all the poison out of their brains – I earn sans funnels, lead magnets, squeeze pages, auto responders and all the other bullshit snake oil old school nonsense – I CAN'T HELP YOU – good luck, you keep chasing the those shiny objects – if you are serious about earning and scaling then rule #1 STOP SELLING and start engaging – but you'll continue your same NON working smart ways – that's so bad.

Me: Google Ads is YouTube Ads.

RF: No they're not. Yes they are all under the Google account – I'm not talking search display or click BID ads that's the road to hell. On YouTube you can run ads on your competitors channel – GET IT? The targeted viewer has already qualified themselves to be in your wheelhouse.

Me: Yes, I know, I run YouTube ads.

RF: Huge difference between Tube videos ads and Google click ads. Oh but you're trying to sell something rather than offer value. Look we are going back and forth – lets agree to disagree. My platform works and drives engaging traffic and that's why I'm overlooking Central Park and you aren't.

Me: I believe I've seen you posting about your YouTube example with the $20 with the 1 cent views, but never seen the case study. Would be happy to watch it, but the insults, posturing and salesmanship are wearing thin and I've got trading stuff to do for tomorrow.

RF: Not trying to sell you anything - we were done yesterday – you have your chance – not interested in working with you – too much baggage in your head – be well – SEE YA!

{nope doesn't end here either}

RF: I had 127 people already sign up for my platform since your first message to me – like I said I CAN'T HELP YOU ANYMORE!

RF: @ $897 per signup – do the math.

Me: Look dude, I get it you are trying to sell your package, good for you... I asked a simple question about your FB ad strategy...that's it, I'm not buying your 5 site package.

RF: I'm not selling. I would have simply educated how I run ads that convert. I'm not your dude – what is this the 70's.

RF: But you never called and as of yesterday we are D O N E!

Me: You mind if I share this conversation with a few friends? This is beyond belief?

{Now it ends…he blocked me}

Rob Anspach

Chapter 12

Psychos Galore

"Good thing Mr. Sarcasm is here to save us."

Arrogant AF

Received a request for a quote early morning July 4th through Facebook chat.

I didn't respond until the next day.

Get a response back from the person seeking a quote, *"we found someone else."*

Me: You know yesterday was a holiday and most businesses took the time to be with family.

Them: Well if you would have responded right away you might have gotten the job, instead we agreed to pay another company $200 a month.

Me: Wow, so glad I didn't respond, that's not even worth our time.

Them: So glad we didn't give it to you then, you sound arrogant AF.

Me: I am. But I also value my time, and my team member's time and you aren't worth the aggravation, but this conversation will be added to my next book.

Them: Yeah well, I'm giving you a nasty review on Yelp.

Me: Okay here's what I want you to post to Yelp, "Owner is arrogant AF," and make sure you use your real profile.

Them: You are arrogant.

Me: We've already established that.

Them: I just don't see why you can't give me a quote.

Me: Well…

(1) you have zero patience,
(2) you want instant follow up on a holiday,
(3) you're rude,
(4) you're cheap AF and
(5) you are not a good fit.

Them: F-You.

Me: Was that F-You on 1, 2, 3, 4 or 5 individually or all of them combined?

Them: All of them and you'd better not put me in a book.

Me: There's no pictures or pop-ups in my books so I'm sure you will never read them anyway.

Them: What the hell? You don't know me.

Me: Well, I did look at your website and there's lots of spelling and grammar errors, and if you paid someone to build that site a year ago and you okayed it, that tells me you can't read very well.

Them: F- You.

Me: You already said that.

{and I got blocked}

30 minutes later...

{received message from Facebook saying my private chat conversation was hostile and that I could lose my Facebook privileges if I continue my aggressive behavior.}

Note: Oh, and apparently you can't jokingly say you're going to throat punch someone on Facebook either. How do I know? I got thrown into Facebook jail for 24 hours.

Reality Check

Hey Rob I know it's last minute but could you {shares what they need done}.

Me: Before I respond...how long did you know you needed to have this done?

Them: Well...3 weeks ago. But, we were busy.

Me: Okay here's my fee {tosses out a ridiculous figure}.

Them: That seems high.

Me: Well it is.

Them: Why?

Me: To pay for the therapy I'm going to need to cope with your last minute cavalier attitude.

Them: That's rude. You can't talk to people like that.

Me: Hmm, many "Rob Versus" books says I can.

Them: What?

Me: Where have you been that you don't know about my "Rob Versus" books?

Them: No idea, but can you help us?

Me: Doubtful.

Them: Why did we even call you?

Me: Ooh, I know this one...the Universe thought you needed a reality check and here I am.

{wait for it...}

Them: F-You.

Note: It is never a good idea to take on a client who has neglected a project then at the last minute asks for help. This will always result in you being the blame for the project not doing as well as it could have if given more time. So either you decline or you price it high enough to compensate for the hassles you will incur.

Twelve Days Is All It Took

A quick disclaimer before I share this story: I have not now nor have I ever asked *"is your spouse a psycho a-hole"* as a preliminary question before accepting a client.

Now that we got that out of the way let's continue...

Just 12 days!

Yep, that was the length of time this particular client went from signing up with our services to being fired and told to never contact us again.

Oh, it started out great.

No red flags.

Nothing that would indicate this client was off-kilter.

In my initial consultation call I spoke with the client for about 45 minutes, she explained that she wasn't happy with her previous marketer. And since we came highly recommended she wanted us to do whatever was necessary to increase her company's presence in the marketplace.

So I created a plan.

Submitted it.

Got the clients approval.

She paid upfront.

Her social media engagement was dismal at best so we tackled that first. The first six days of posts engagement took off. Then it happened.

I got a chat message...

"Hi, I'm not happy with the direction you are taking with the social media. I wasn't informed that you were hired and I think before you proceed you should contact me to discuss."

That message didn't come from the client.

It came from the client's husband who didn't even work for the company.

So I called the client to explain the message. She informed me that it was her husband that happened to be the person doing the previous marketing. And he wasn't a marketer nor did he understand marketing and I was to ignore him.

After 5 days, there was now more engagement on their business Facebook page than the previous 2 months. Then I got an email.

Yup, it was the husband again.

He was demanding I contact him.

I ignore it.

Then 6 hours later another email. Followed by another one an hour later. So I respond...

"I was not hired by you. You don't even work for the company. I have no obligation to respond to any message you send me. So stop contacting me."

Well apparently that must have set him off and an hour later I received a voice call from the client asking me to politely work with her husband and to make changes to the marketing. *"With all due respect"*, I said... *"your husband's an a-hole."*

And he happened to be listening in.

To which he started screaming.

So I hung up.

Then he went in and removed all the posts we had scheduled on the clients Facebook page for the rest of the month (even though it was getting great engagement and driving traffic).

That's when I contacted the client and told her I was firing her.

Well, that happened a year ago. I don't know if it was the marriage or Covid or something else...but that former client is no longer in operation.

What do you think? Should I ask that question from now on?

Me, Be Serious, Pfft!

Rob, you should be more serious.

{message I received thru Facebook chat}

Me: Why?

Them: You would get more business.

Me: I have plenty of business.

Them: Well you would get even more.

Me: I take on clients who appreciate me for who I am.

Them: That's ridiculous. You're too sarcastic.

Me: Duh!

Them: See, right there, you could have been more diplomatic with your answer.

Me: Why?

Them: Well your sarcasm turns people off.

Me: Which people?

Them: Well, me for one.

Me: You should lighten up...stop being so serious.

{wait for it...}

Them: F-You.

Me: Congrats you have just been inducted into my next book.

Them: Book, what are you talking about?

Me: Have you been living in a cave?

Them: What are you talking about?

Me: I would think by now anyone who follows me on FB and sends me a chat message knows I write books and that I have a whole series called "Rob Versus" where I share my adventures with scammers, morons, lousy customer service and idiots who waste my time.

Them: Are you calling me a moron.

Me: Did I say that? But since you assumed.

{wait for it again....}

Them: F-You.

Me: You seem to like that word.

Them: Go away.

Me: You sent me a chat first, so you go away.

Them: I'm reporting you.

Me: Dude, you can't report me for a chat you initiated.

Them: I'm doing it anyway.

Me: Okay, I'll wait.

Them: FB will suspend you.

Me: Did you do it yet?

Them: Shut up and go away.

Me: So, you still want me to be serious?

{third times a charm...}

Them: F-You.

{and I got blocked}

Note: Being serious is boring. Complying with someone's wish to be boring is insane. Sharing someone's interaction about my refusal to be boring is priceless.

When They Try To Recruit Me

Hey Rob, we'd love for you to come work for us.

Me: What's it pay?

Them: {tosses out a number}

Me: Sure, as long as I'm only required to work one hour per day.

Them: No, we require you to work a full day.

Me: Well, based on the amount you quoted my full day would be 60 minutes.

Them: We require at least 8 hours from you per day.

Me: Then your salary to me will need to be 8 times higher.

Them: That's not how it works.

Me: If you want to hire me, that's exactly how it works.

Them: We don't have the budget for it.

Me: Here's my solution, if they fire you, along with some of the other dead weight then they could afford to hire me.

{they hung up}

Note: I'm not really looking, I'm happy being the guy in charge at Anspach Media, but I get these calls frequently from companies who think they can recruit me. It never ends well for them.

It Finally Happened

YESSSS! FINALLY!

An electric scammer calls me and goes into his script about how he can save me 30% off my electric rate... he asks me who my electric supplier is...

I say: HWP (which if you read my books stands for Hamster Wheel Powered).

He asks me to repeat that.

I say again: HWP.

{there's a short pause}

So I ask if there is a problem.

Scammer: Does HWP stand for Hamster Wheel Powered?

Me: Darn skippy it does.

Scammer: You're that guy!

Me: What guy?

Scammer: The guy who wastes our time and puts us in his books.

Me: You got me.

Then I hear a loud "F-YOU" as if the whole call center said it in unison.

Then he hung up.

You know it really made my day and a very touching end to a scam call.

About The Author

Rob is affectionately known as "Mr. Sarcasm" to his friends - to everyone else he's a Certified Digital Marketing Strategist, a Foremost Expert On Specialized SEO, a Serial Author, Podcaster, Speaker and Authority Broadcaster who can help amplify YOU to your audience.

Rob has also produced books for many clients including lawyers, doctors, copywriters, speakers and consultants.

Rob helps companies across the globe generate new revenue and capture online business. And he hates scammers with a passion.

Rob is available to share talks and give interviews.

To learn more about Rob visit **www.AnspachMedia.com** or call Anspach Media at **(412)267-7224** today.

About The Contributors

Adam Hommey is the author of Groundhog Day is an Event, Not a Business Strategy, and a contributing author to Journeys to Success: The Millennial Edition – both international Amazon best-sellers. He has spoken on stages around the country for many years and is a sought-after expert on podcasting for entrepreneurs. Adam is also the founder of Everything Podcasting™ www.everythingpodcasting.group

Gerry Oginski is a NY Medical Malpractice & Personal Injury Attorney in practice for 32 years. He has created over 3200 videos to help consumers in New York understand how medical malpractice and accident lawsuits work. He is the author of four consumer-oriented books: Secrets of a NY Medical Malpractice Attorney, Doctors Gone Wild, In Case of Death and Beyond the ER Doors.
To learn more about Gerry, visit https://Oginski-Law.com
To see some of Gerry's informative videos, visit
https://www.youtube.com/c/GerryOginski10

Mia Oginski is a graduate of University of Delaware and hopes to enter law school in the near future. She has a similar sense of humor as her dad and has totally embraced the Rob Anspach method of Scamming the Scammers. She eagerly devours each new book and patiently awaits new scam calls leaving her in stitches each time.

Courtney Beauford is a kick-ass Las Vegas real estate expert specializing in traditional and distressed residential properties. As a former "military brat", Courtney loves to help active-duty and retired military find their dream homes. On a personal level, Courtney enjoys riding his Harley and competing in Brazilian Jiu-Jitsu. To buy or sell a home visit Courtney at: https://courtneybeauford.chime.me

Kirt Christensen has been a stock trader for 22 plus years and teaches others to do the same...get a free, educational, 40 minute training at: https://stocktradingscience.com/sts-webinar

Resources

THE INTERVIEW SERIES FOR ENTREPRENEURS

Rob Anspach interviews talented entrepreneurs who demonstrate an eagerness to share their experiences, their knowledge and their stories to help others succeed.

Listen to the Rob Anspach's E-Heroes Podcast today.

Available on:

Apple, Google, I Heart Radio, Stitcher, Spotify, Pandora

Or

www.AnspachMedia.com

Rob Versus The Scammers

Protecting The World Against Fraud, Nuisance Calls & Downright Phony Scams.

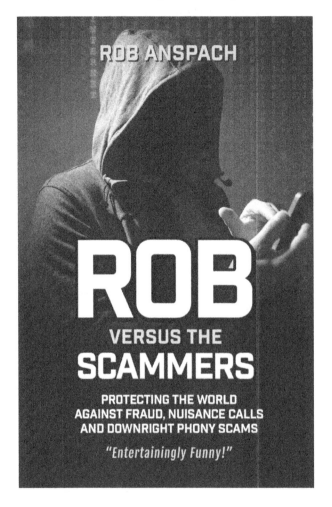

Available on Amazon in Print & Kindle or at…
www.RobVersusTheScammers.com

Rob Versus The Morons

Overcoming Idiotic Customers With Wit, Sarcasm And A Take No Bullshit Attitude

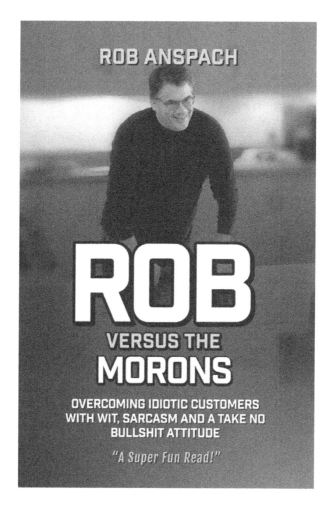

**Available on Amazon in Print & Kindle
or at…
www.RobVersusTheMorons.com**

Rob Versus Humanity

The Last Line Of Defense In Outwitting, Outlasting and Outliving Time Wasters, Fraudsters And Fools.

Available on Amazon in Print & Kindle or at...
www.RobVersusHumanity.com

Rob Versus The Entitled

Defeating The Aggressive, Offended, And Easily Triggered With A Little Common Sense & A Lot Of Sarcasm.

Available on Amazon in Print & Kindle or at…
www.RobVersusTheEntitled.com

Other Books By Rob Anspach

Available on Amazon in Print & Kindle.

www.amazon.com/author/robertanspach

Books Produced By
Anspach Media
That You Might Enjoy

To learn more visit https://AnspachMedia.com/books

I'll Leave You With This...

While I was out of town my dad called me saying he received a call from what sounded like my son.

Caller: *Grandpa I was in an accident, I have a broken nose and being cited with DUI. The person I hit was a pregnant women who was taken to intensive care, can you help?*

My dad responded with, *"let me call your parents"*.

The caller hung up.

My dad then called me.

I called my son who was at home, safe and sound.

No accident, no broken nose and no injured pregnant woman.

Please share with your parents, grandparents and neighbors and let them know if they receive phone calls from what sounds like children, grandchildren, nieces or nephews to...

    (1) always ask questions
    (2) get as much details as possible
    (3) never agree to give out credit card or banking info
       and
    (4) call relatives and/or law enforcement and let them
       know about the call.

Reviews Continued…

"My dad, Gerry Oginski, introduced me to Rob's books. I had always received spam calls— I was quick to roll my eyes, block, and press decline. After reading the Rob Versus books, and drawing a ton of inspiration from them, I now eagerly await scam calls. Just last week I told a scammer that my name was Luz Ázol (read it quickly and you'll understand), and that my credit card expiration date was 14/36. I could not have done it without my dad and Rob— and I love my new hobby! It will not disappoint." – **Mia Oginski**

"This compilation of short stories may lead you to believe that Rob is a social media jerk, rude and unprofessional.... but in reality that is not the case. In reality, he is a super smart direct marketer, a family man, a personal and professional friend to many and a JOY to work and play with. This book is NOT about Rob. This funny book is about protecting your autonomy, defining your rules of engagement and doing business ONLY with people who are willing to work and play with you the way you want them to. Rob protects his freedom of choice, his freedom of time, his freedom of relationships, his freedom of process. We should do it too. Of all Rob's books, while this is most funniest and easiest to read... this has the deepest meaning and it teaches a very valuable life lesson. THIS IS HOW I CHOOSE TO OPERATE, IF YOU DON'T LIKE IT, THAT IS OK, BUT YOU CAN'T BE HERE ANYMORE. Yes the book is hilarious and a JOY to read... but that is just expected from Rob. God sent Rob on earth to make busy entrepreneurs SMILE. Reading this book was my two hour vacation and it was fun." ~ ***Parthiv Shah***, www.elaunchers.com

"My ribs hurt from laughing so hard. Rob did it again. Sarcasm and humor in a book you can't put down."
~ **Brad Szollose**, Host of Awakened Nation

"Been driving all day from Vegas to Idaho. More than half of which we have had to tolerate a crying 9 month old. On the bright side I have almost finished your book. Just can't do that with the kid crying. I have laughed out loud quite a few times." ~ **Erik Olson**, https://carpetcleaningboise.com

"*Rob Anspach recently posted a friend request he had received where there was no photo of the person sending the request. His question was, "What are the chances I accept this connection?" Now, most people said, "no way!" but, I know Rob, so I responded, "Well, you knowingly answer spam phone calls just to give them a hard time, so I'd say the chances are extremely high and we'll see the results in a new book soon!" If you are a scammer you do not want your path to cross with Rob. As he shows in his latest book, Rob takes a no-holds-barred approach when it comes to dealing with these Whackadoos. And he enjoys making a game out of it, often causing people to call him rude and hang up on him. Rob does what most of us have thought about doing, but don't have the patience or the guts to actually do it – calling people out for being scam artists. If you are looking for a little levity and want to bring some laughter to your day, read this book (then go back and read his other books in this series). Mr. Sarcasm has done it again!"*
~**Greg Jameson**

"*No one teaches daily lessons through sarcasm like Rob Anspach. I'm guessing that this is because he's a man of few words, and prefers to let his wit do the talking for him.*"
~ **Lindy & Matt Denny**, *www.MohawkMattDenny.com*

"*Rob Anspach has done it again! His unique writing style portrays the reality of his conversations as if you were a fly on the wall. I can hear his voice and I can hear the poor "other side" as they sink deeper and deeper into submission to Rob's brilliant sarcasm. It's awesome to see he's pulled it off yet again in "Rob vs the Whackadoos". And I've picked up one or two things I'm going to try - not the least of which is his Auto Reply email loop! Don't ever stop answering your phone, Rob!*"
~ **Pam Prior**, https://www.ProfitConcierge.com/

"*Rob VS The Whackadoos did not disappoint. It's amazing the way Rob threads the lesson through a story, injecting just the right amount of humor and sarcasm... he is THE KING OF SARCASM... and the book is the best yet! I think we all know a Whackadoo or two. Read it. You're welcome.*" – **Sherry Hemstreet**

"I am a huge fan of Rob and his books starting with Rob Versus The Scammers. As I read every one of his stories in his most recent book, I couldn't help but laugh out loud and relate to exactly the scenarios he discussed.

His comments are on point, sarcastic and intended for those unfortunate scammers who clearly don't realize they are in over their head every time they invite him to press one for more information or to learn how to reduce his payments.

One of my all-time favorites is the name of his electric company clearly designed to have you laughing in stitches when you realize that the person calling has no clue what the name of the company represents and doesn't realize his sole purpose is to waste their time.

The book will put a smile on your face and give you great ideas the next time somebody calls you to reduce your card payments or lower your interest-rate. If you haven't done so already I highly recommend reading each of his other books. That will give you a true insight into Rob's truly sarcastic and creative mind and make you appreciate all the time he wastes with these awful scammers.

I loved reading this book so much I shared it with my daughter who couldn't stop laughing and has applied Rob's methods and strategies each time she receives these time wasting calls.

I highly recommend this book." ~ **Gerry Oginski**

If you enjoyed reading this book, I would encourage you to leave a review on Amazon. Leaving reviews helps others decide if my book (or any author's book) is worth their time to read. It just takes a few minutes and your review could be the deciding factor in convincing someone to pick up a book and take an adventure.

~ Rob

Remember to…

Share This Book!

Share it with your friends!

Share it with your colleagues!

Share it with law enforcement!

Share it on social media.

Share it using this hashtag...

#RobVersusTheWhackadoos

Made in the USA
Monee, IL
19 December 2021

86436006R00085